Let's Talk About
STEALING

Let's Talk About
STEALING

By JOY BERRY

Illustrated by John Costanza
Edited by Orly Kelly
Designed by Jill Losson

GROLIER ENTERPRISES CORP.

Let's talk about STEALING.

Has someone ever taken something of yours and not returned it?

STEALING is taking and keeping something that does not belong to you. When you take and keep something that belongs to another person, you are STEALING.

Whenever someone steals something from you —

- you may feel disappointed, frustrated, and angry;
- you may think that you cannot trust the person;
- you may not want the person to be around your things.

It is important to treat other people the way you want to be treated.

If you do not want other people to steal from you, you must not steal from them.

Some people *steal accidentally.*

This happens when they do not return something that they have borrowed.

Or it happens when people take something without thinking about it.

When you find out that you have accidentally stolen something, return it right away.

Some people *steal on purpose.* They know what they are doing. They choose to steal.

Sometimes people steal because they want something, or they might think that they *need* it.

Sometimes people steal because *their friends steal*. They may think that it is OK to steal because their friends do it.

They might not want to be different from their friends who steal.

Maybe they think that their friends will like them more if they steal.

Some people steal because *they think that it will not make a difference.* They think that no one will notice. They tell themselves that it will not hurt anyone.

Some people steal because *they are angry.* They may want to get back at someone who did something to hurt them.

It does not make any difference why people steal. *Stealing is wrong.* It is never OK to take and keep something that does not belong to you.

If you should steal something, do something about it right away. If you have not damaged or destroyed the thing you have stolen, return it.

If you have damaged or destroyed the thing you have stolen, replace it or pay for it.

After you have returned or replaced what you have stolen, *say that you are sorry* and *try not to steal again.*

It is important to treat other people the way you want to be treated.

If you do not want other people to steal from you, you must not steal from them.